MARION JONES

DISCOVER THE LIFE OF A SPORTS STAR II

David and Patricia Armentrout

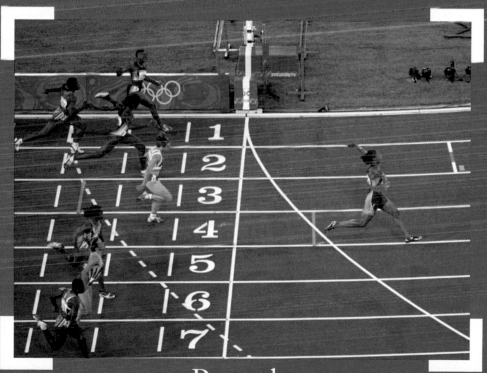

Rourke
Publishing LLC
Vero Beach, Florida 32964

www.rourkepublishing.com

PHOTO CREDITS:
Cover, Page 19 ©Andy Lyons/Getty Images; Cover, Page 15 ©Mike Powell/Getty Images; Title Page ©Ross Kinnaird/Getty Images; Page 8 ©Jamie McDonald/Getty Images; Page 17 ©Mark Thompson/Allsport; Page 10 ©Allsport UK/Allsport; Page 18©Gary M. Prior/Getty Images; Page 4 ©Marco Rosi/LaPresse; Page 14 ©Tony Duff/Allsport; Pages 5, 7 ©Devissi/Prestige/Newsmakers; Page 12 ©Doug Pensinger/Allsport; Page 21 ©Adam Pretty/Allsport

Title page: *Marion Jones reacts emotionally after crossing the finish line to win the gold medal in the women's 100-meter final at the 2000 Olympics.*

Editor: Frank Sloan

Cover and interior design by Nicola Stratford

Library of Congress Cataloging-in-Publication Data

Armentrout, David, 1962-
  Marion Jones / David and Patricia Armentrout.
    p. cm. -- (Discover the life of a sports star II)
  Includes bibliographical references and index.
  ISBN 1-59515-131-1 (hardcover)
  1. Jones, Marion, 1975---Juvenile literature. 2. Runners (Sports)--United States--Biography--Juvenile literature. 3. Women runners--United States--Biography--Juvenile literature. I. Armentrout, Patricia, 1960- II. Title. II. Series: Armentrout, David, 1962- Discover the life of a sports star II.
  GV1061.15.J67A76 2004
  796.42'2'092--dc22
                                                        2004007639

Printed in the USA

CG/CG

Table of Contents

Marion wins the bronze in the women's long jump in Sydney.

Marion Jones

Marion Jones is an Olympic champion and one of the fastest women on Earth. She has more will and determination than most people. When Marion sets out to accomplish a goal, nothing stands in her way.

Born: October 12, 1975 in Los Angeles, California
Height: 5′ 11″ (1.6 m)
Weight: 150 pounds (68 kg)
Events: Sprints and Long Jump
Record: First female track and field athlete to win five medals in a single Olympics

Marion's Family

Marion was born in 1975 to Marion and George Jones. Marion did not know her birth father because he left the family when she was very young.

Marion's mother later married Ira Toler. Marion had a good relationship with her stepfather. Tragically, Ira died of a stroke when Marion was 11, and Marion was left without a father again.

Marion enjoys media attention with her mother and uncle while attending a sports gala.

Marion was always eager to compete against the boys, and win!

Keeping up with the Boys

Marion liked to play with her stepbrother Albert. She spent a lot of time chasing him and his friends around the neighborhood. Marion was much younger than the boys, but she had no trouble keeping up with them. It was clear that Marion had a talent for running fast.

Flo Jo celebrates her 100-m win at the 1988 Olympic Games in Seoul, Korea.

Inspired by Flo Jo

Marion watched Florence Griffith-Joyner, or Flo Jo, in the 1988 Olympics on television. Flo Jo competed in **athletics**, also known as track and field. She set world records in the 100- and 200-meter events (10.49 seconds and 21.34 seconds), and became the fastest woman in the world. Flo Jo retired after the Olympics and died in 1998. She still holds the world record in those events.

Marion was inspired by Flo Jo's performance and later wrote, "I want to be an Olympic champion" on the school blackboard.

On the basketball court against the
Virginia Cavaliers in 1994

School Sports

Marion competed in high school track and was already one of the fastest **sprinters** in the world. She set a national high school record in 1991. She ran the 200-meter in 22.76 seconds. Marion was named High School Athlete of the Year by *Track and Field News*.

Marion was also very talented on the basketball court. She averaged 22.8 points per game her senior year. She earned a basketball scholarship to the University of North Carolina. Marion helped the Tarheels win the **NCAA** championship her freshman year.

Fastest Woman in the World!

In 1997, Marion decided to quit basketball and focus on track. Marion had a new coach, Trevor Graham, who helped her improve her times. That year she won U.S titles in the 100-meter and the Long Jump. At the World championships in Athens, Marion won the gold for the 100-meter (10.83 seconds) and became the fastest woman in the world!

Marion competes in a college track meet.

Marion crosses the finish line and wins the gold at the World Championships in Athens, Greece.

Personal Bests

Marion set personal bests at the World Cup in 1998. She finished the 100-meter in 10.65 seconds and the 200-meter in 21.62 seconds.

Marion also ranked first in the world in the 100- and 200-meter races and third in the Long Jump in 1999.

Hard work and determination win Marion her personal best in the 100-meter race.

Sweet success for Marion at the 2000 Olympic Games

Five-time Olympic Medalist

Marion set out to win five gold medals at the 2000 Olympic Games in Sydney, Australia. Marion won gold in three events, the 100-, 200-, and 4x400-meter relays. She won bronze in the Long Jump and the 4x100 relay. Marion did not get her five gold medals, but she made history. She became the first female track and field athlete to win five medals in a single Olympics. The **IAAF** named Marion Athlete of the Year.

Marion is on her way to victory as she carries a purple baton in the 400-meter relay in Sydney.

Continuing on the Fast Track

Marion was the 200-meter (22.39 seconds) World champ in 2001. She finished her 2002 season undefeated for the first time in her career. Marion did not compete in 2003. She gave birth to her son, Tim, in June.

Marion is eager to compete at the 2004 Olympics in Athens, Greece. Her ultimate goal, however, is to be mentioned among other great athletes such as Michael Jordan, Pelé, and Muhammad Ali.

Marion proudly displays the American flag.

Dates to Remember

1975	Born in Los Angeles, California
1988	Is inspired by Florence Griffith-Joyner
1997	Becomes the fastest woman in the world
1998	Sets personal records in the 100- and 200-meter races
2000	Wins five medals at the Olympic Games in Sydney
2001	World 200-meter champion
2002	Has her first undefeated season
2003	Son Tim is born

Glossary

athletics (ath LET iks) — competitive sports that involve running, jumping, or throwing, also known as track and field events

IAAF International Association of Athletics Federations — The governing body for organized athletic competition programs held all over the world, from world competitions to national and local events

NCAA National Collegiate Athletic Association — A group of colleges, universities, and other athletic groups who establish programs to govern and promote athletics

sprinters (SPRINT erz) — short-distance racers

USATF USA Track and Field — The national governing body for track and field, long-distance running, and race walking

Index

Further Reading

Feldman, Heather. *Marion Jones: World Class Runner.* Powerkids Press, 2003.
Rapoport, Ron. *See How She Runs: Marion Jones and the Making of a Champion.* Algonquin Books, 2000.
Gutman, Bill. *Marion Jones: The Fastest Runner in the World.* Simon Pulse, 2000.
Emerson, Carl. *Marion Jones.* Childs World, 2001.

Websites To Visit

www.usatf.org/
www.iaaf.org/

About The Authors

David and Patricia Armentrout have written many nonfiction books for young readers. They have had several books published for primary school reading. The Armentrouts live in Cincinnati, Ohio, with their two children.